Never a Child

Never a Child

Poems

M.A. Mahadeo

N, O₂ N,
CANADA

Publisher's note: This book is a work of fiction. Names, characters, places and incidents are either the product of the author's imagination or are used fictitiously, and any resemblance to actual persons living or dead is entirely coincidental.

LIBRARY AND ARCHIVES CANADA CATALOGUING IN PUBLICATION

Title: Never a child : poems / M.A. Mahadeo.

Names: Mahadeo, M. A., 1994– author.

Identifiers: Canadiana 20200168630 | ISBN 9781988098999 (softcover)

Classification: LCC PS8626.A37585 N48 2020 | DDC C811/.6—dc23

Printed and bound in Canada on 100% recycled paper.

NOW OR NEVER PUBLISHING
901, 163 Street
Surrey, British Columbia
Canada V4A 9T8

NONPUBLISHING.COM
Fighting Words.

We gratefully acknowledge the support of the Canada Council for the Arts and the British Columbia Arts Council for our publishing program.

September 04, 2016
To my Laila

About Modern Poetry

I ask, I know it's true.
You want me to build on something,
I can barely. . .

Is this what you want?

A profound statement from me—
a *feminist* statement and you with red dark eyes pitter-pattering over me.
Wiping off the comments with the screams
that shake me all over.

You feel empowered as trembling souls within me grasp out to you,
you say,
"Say it,"
with the applause you're giving me.

Is this what you want?

You want my poems to be of an attack—almost a child ago,
holding her underneath our ruffled skirts.
Beware children the ghost will proclaim,
as you latch onto your false pretension within the ironclad chains you've forged.
A heavy memory you've locked the key unto me.

Is this what you want?

I beg to understand the importance of me
being strong
being victim
being brave
and yet . . .

I give you what you want.

Thus, the cycle continues, until we learn the rules to break it.

Stutter

The first time I began to stutter was at my grandfather's funeral,
choking on p's and q's during a speech for a man,
the Man I barely knew.

I tried everything from an anthology of movies
to cure just the anxiety of my shaking throat.
Joining a Catholic choir,
a Catholic chime choir,
changing to a different Catholic school.
It became quite evident Jesus was not going to cure
my anxiety mouth.

When I met my man . . .
The nerves of my heart,
pushing out to force my bakes,
into place like the amount of foundation on my skin.
I was slayed to the, not god,
when it came to speech I was telling him.

Looking in my eyes,
he asked, "How are you?"
I was happy that I was unable to say anything at all other than
scare him with the vertebrae of my
hissing noise.

The constant search,
the constant noise,
the constant stutter,
found silence.

Walking into the room
with everyone who was apparently just as nervous as I was.
They, allowing their vibrations to take over their voice . . .
Everyone was stuttering speech,
with our constant noise,
of,
Om.

I Was Never A Child

I was never a child the moment I grew up was around the age
of somewhere between one and eighteen.
I was told by teachers
in the rural notion,
"You can't just be sad over nothing or everything!"

Taking this to heart,
taking this to sleeve,
and taking the blood off of my arms,
I was never a child.

I was never a child,
the moment I knew what
affair meant.
And how the innocent experience,
of what I was doing
meant that everything was my fault
and that the excuse of simple childhood meant hiding my diary
under my bed.

I still do that,
I still can't come to name you.

I was never a child.
Hiding bloodied underwear under socks and garments
to keep my teller in secret,
knowing they would get mad over spilt,
Womanhood.

Every girl knows the secret to this hiding.
Yet, knowing the secret of soap and cold water as a teen,
fearing for your own,
and the dreaded idea of,
"Grow up!"

I was never a child.
Feeling my arms extending to the empty room and empty words of,
"We're so proud of you."

But I was never a child,
even though I was always
and forever,
a woman.

Praying

When I was younger, I was always praying.
Praying to the God who would give me blessings,
through the religion classes my universe forced me to sit through.

When I was younger, I was always asking,
more or less,
of Jesus and his blessings to reign down to something
other than miscommunication.

I ain't never ate meat on a Friday for him to make me
skinny and give,
give the one thing I needed in high school,
a prom-date.

I asked Jesus
for a boyfriend so many times.
The back log of my prayers were behind the voices
who actually needed them.

'Cause I never heard back,
nothing.

I stopped believing in anything and I knew he wasn't listening.
Only sitting up in his high throne,
pretending to be on the right side.
As was I,
the left side of history,
in a town which flew flags flown by Devils,
as they called themselves, "right wing."

I stopped them prayers,
even when I saw the lamb in the field
and a snake beneath my ankles,
waiting.

When I met the one,
but, the first love that was right,
he smiled at me in the window.

He looked at me with brown filled eyes.
I asked him what he wanted for dinner,
and he said coyly,
"chicken is fine,"
and bells went off in my head.
He said, "I love you,"
and I didn't even need to say it back,
but I did anyway.

My teller asking,
"Well, where did you meet him? He's different?"

And I never again asked Jesus for an answer,
as I was the one fixing my own questions.

The love of my life,
and the carrier of my heart was in that window.
My prayers had been answered
all this time,

and I make sure to thank Krishna, by all his names,
everyday.

Opaque

I was going to be opaque for the rest of time.
No matter the look of my outside,
opaque with the words no one in
my village
knew I was saying.

Among the basic people who threw parties in grass,
as I was walking amongst the corn stalks.
Nails stolen from the drug store,
and my going out clothes
were my sister's hand-me-down Church attire.

Opaque where people looked right through me,
or tried to.
The country past-time,
meaning that my drug of choice was green—
yet the levels
of upper-middle class,
were still looming above my head.

Losing respect for titles,
when low, is still higher than you.

And now I don't claim to be anything other than a shade of white.
Looking still throughout the privilege of my feet,
I am the souls of these feet.

But for 18 years,
I was opaque.

Mistake

As I grabbed the blanket off of the clean room,
where my teller's knuckles were red with the blood of hard work.
Watching a *reality* show they'd looked at me,
saying,
"I would go crazy, that room just isn't clean."
Because that was the grossest part,
about *reality*.

Knowing it was more than just grabbing the blanket
off of the clean room,
"YOU ARE A MISTAKE!"
Screaming from the person who I assumed meant it in the way,
I was born into cleanliness, purity: mess it up, messed it up.

We would clean the house every Saturday morning.
Hours,
upon hours. Clean, clean.
Ironic, my family.
A farmer who gave back to the Earth,
was tied to an action who cleaned.

Cleaned,
Cleaned,
with chemicals.
Now, I fear they might get into my eyes—
clean to blind, erase.
How many times, without ripping off my own personality,
afraid the washing was of me.

Mistake,
of taking a blanket off.
Unraveling it
around my body to sleep in a clean room.
I had made the notion

that the room,
the home was meant to be lived in.
When in all reality,
it was never clean to begin with.

Mistake of living,
where the actions of my childhood were covered in the mud of
how I was different.
I wrapped the blanket around me
in a room not meant for warmth.

They took it away, slapped my wrist,
and told me
to stop making messes.
"Go play outside!"
Finally, where the dirt from my shoes, the dirt from my soul
could roam free.

To the First Man Who Called Me Beautiful

The first
Man to ever call me beautiful shall tell my daughters,
"Your eyes,
Like my wife,
Shine bright."

Beauty in the eyes of my
lover.
Beautiful,
as he did not need to prove he was a
Man.

In Dirt

I was always playing in dirt,
always.
Running through it,
not noticing that my pretend jewelry,
just a costume, manicure becoming grey.
Glued on, acrylic didn't come with a health note.
Ripped off the first layer, opening up.

I was always playing in dirt.
Throwing it up into the air,
where no one, not the neighbors five miles away couldn't hear.

The country where everyone was knowing of someone,
but knew no one living in the city.

It wasn't until I left to the ocean and lakeside when I began to play
with mud.

We Were All in Lines

All of the girls were all in lines to talk to the guidance
counselor.

The woman,
who would help us through,
our own -ish.

We were all in lines.
All in a row waiting for her "guidance counselor" advice,
which we would ignore anyways.
Spreading lies
to avoid the truth of what was happening at home, at school,
and in our own universe. Ignored.

We were all in lines.
This girl had this,
that girl had that and the man behind the principal's desk
only called us the lady team.
Instead of giving us more attention,
and not popping pills as the cool kids smoked in the valley.

We were all in lines.
Hiding from the truth of the fact,
that maybe if someone would listen rather than judge us
for not cheering
on the team on nights, with lights—
then our sixteen years would not have gone to waste.

We were all in lines, just waiting for counseling.
If only they would have noticed the lines upon my wrists,
praying.
That we were seeking
help, and not counsel.

Drug

I experimented.
Only in high school with drugs and then with medicine,
but which was which?
Which could help the mind of a questioning,
depression?

The drug of choice was filled inside a circular prison
behind the bars of my mind.
And the laughing medicine,
I found in the park behind the prison of the police,
who really shouldn't have eaten so many donuts.

There wasn't much else to do, other than to toke up rather
than popping. Afraid to leave the house. I felt comfortable
within four walls.
My teller claiming,
"I would do it and leave for my parents,"
as I was rushed out of the door with a dime bag of suppressants.

Filling lungs with love and brain with destruction.
The abyss of my body,
like a claw.
I was trying to reach out and in the moments of breathing I felt
free from the money line.
The line everyone closer to the Southern Island forgot about.

But it was accepted to kill my brain, pop them to concentrate.
And atomic bombs to fill my lungs with the herb
that would once allow me now,
to see God.

Running Through Corn

The tats,
the tears,
the feeling of bounce beneath my feet and hills rolling.
As much as I was rolling earth's herb
in between thumb and pointer finger,
after through corn.

I ran where I could find,
keeping up with my minute per mind.
After sitting in testimony thinking of the face,
of the boy, the child, the never to be man
without innocence and his lawyer.
Privilege surrounding the arena,
a spectator—a man asking,
"Well, why couldn't you kick and scream him off?"

Thinking to myself with hate for the cage for my aura.

A thought that now I fight with every single fiber of my heart.
When sixteen-year-old girls can't fight
because the fibers of our heart aren't strong enough yet. Beaten
down by the idea of potential, and the never-ending, judge.

The strength in my ability to run away.
I put feet on with lightning bolts.
The Roman in me and the violence of Mercury flowing
through my blood,
I was now angry enough to pace miles.
I finally ran through the corn which once cut me.
The corn which once challenged my very core,
my very future.
Thinking that it could slice me with the nature,
my father had planted.

The corn persisted,
the corn I rocked down,
with the dust my stride created.
A God among the thoughts I now controlled—
I ran to the beat of the sweet humming noise that my future
would teach me,
without knowledge of what to call it.

And the sun's Rays beating down,
would light my way.

Call Melissa

I grew in all different directions.
Up,
down,
inward,
but never outward.

Holding onto my emotions, never seeing a tear fall from my fears.
I grew to hate the name,
Melissa.

It meant,
unfamiliar.
It meant in trouble.
It meant in therapy.
Never a capacity for joy.
It was the name of someone who didn't know me.
Given as a gift, I had to accept like a curse.

Melissa,
was crafted out of teachers who were substitutes
who were calling me talkative.
Because women speaking wasn't a good thing, but meant we were out of order,
out of turn,
and most definitely out of place.
Underneath was the only acceptable.

Melissa,
was crafted out of popular boys and beautiful girls.
Serious girls had no cellulite.
A Renaissance painting stared back at the mirror.
Italian figure, they'd call it.
Nicknames were for people not belonging to the society,

society that loathed to adhere to people's
identity
for which
they
claimed.

"What's your name?"
He looked at me.
My heart sizzling,
"Mimzy." I replied, thinking he would like the funny girl.

"I'll call you Melissa," I didn't blink the minute.
Nor would I ever again.
For the only person who ever knew my eyes,
while his were closed was the man behind the breath
of Melissa.

Dear Teller

I was once on fire.
Yet, you told me,
"Put yourself out,"
with the word
crazy.
Popping,
not listening.

Today I set ablaze where oceans do not
go and
where lakes sprinkle me with just enough oxygen.

May I blaze the seeds of the trees planted,
where you once had held me down.

My Rotis Aren't Round

The little girl behind the roller had absolutely no idea
what she was doing.
Thanksgiving,
American.
But not asking for help when my guide said,
"This is completely wrong."

'07,
I should shake the apples meaning to stir the ingredients together.
Not peeling away their indiscretions,
not washing away their imperfections like I do with myself
today.

Pie.
The ultimate coming of age for the child baker.
I, proud of myself,
offended my teller when she wanted to be the only
female in the kitchen.
I wasn't even allowed to be
learning to grow.

The rise of the dough,
the loss of my steam,
the self I wanted to become.
I grasped ahold of
The Spice,
which contained all of the ingredients.
As my teller threw the food off into the ether,
"You never asked me for help! It's disgusting."

Pie,
the whitest thing I could have done.
Besides drape my jacket over my knees in a Bollywood movie,
I was so close to making the perfect pastry,
Little left of center.

I grab the water bottle, too poor using it as a pin
to smooth out the flour,
water,
and oil over the cast iron.
He, the giver now sits in the living room.
Love match,
strike, fire,
on the stove to heat the dough.

Rise.

Constant flashes of fire across the underside of the pan.
I use too much oil,
I use too much flour,

and my rotis aren't round.

They never will be.

A child who couldn't bake pie.
Me, a woman who couldn't rise dough,
always left of center, and sparks of the food to define me.
The lady whose recipe was neither,
here,
nor over the border.

Pie and rotis never round.
Apples never peeled.
But I will let my daughter know
she is more than just mistakes in the kitchen.

I Never Spoke Italian

A five-year-old asks their elder,
"How come you never spoke Italian?"
With pride stating and looking down,
not equal,
or even across il pasto,
but down,
"Because we are NOW American."

Taking it from the little girl, even the title of being anything but
ripping the idea from her head.
Leaving her an empty shell of where culture had once been placed,
in the vault called hope.

The gentle l's,
the rolling r's,
la mia famiglia e de Palermo,
in the broken-est of all broken
constructions.
Ruining a language more ancient than the gladiators,
"But they speak such broken English?"
The lady would remark.

I heard snippets on broken dreams and broken minds.
When air couldn't reach the right brain cavity
it reverted from the toxic force
of the uprooted lives of Brooklyn.
Through a stroke of the Godfather, Grand,
the patriarch looking at me,
"Bellisima."

The roots run deep through the soils of men who change
our name from D'amato,
disregarding we were from the village.
Simply to Amato,
claiming we owned the entire thing.

My fate was set.
Yet, never did I utter a word hearing on pilgrimage
to the *father*-land,
"E 'nel sangue."
Sei un Amato.

Amato,
to love.
Translated,
I was never the translation of my blood.
The interpretation of who you saw.
A child of not the Tuscan but always outside of the city.
Always.

A girl with a name fated,
to love.
To be loved and meant to be loved.
The blood of something else,
creeping into the understanding of who I was.
The American notion to take the love
away.

The moment I opened my eyes,
I longed again for the love of my last name.
And the love of a people I had to give up.
All for the red Earth,
blue eyes,
and white men who told me that not even the Little Italy
could hold me anymore.

The curse of being removed from beauty
and from my one true love,
te amo.
The land which ran through my soul and the blood of un amate.

Questioning

When I stopped looking for
answers in questions,
realizing it was not my thoughts.

Yet it was the mindfulness which made truth.

We are not the roots of the nursery,
but are the pollen which blow
from wind to
dust.

A Cup of Leaves

Chai
tea
latte.

Chai tea latte.

Chai.

Steeped in bubbles, bath and rum,
you and I watched him dance to Shreya and Udit
among wives.
You understanding the poetry in her eyes.
Lost in love,
our first, of many first dates.

Watching the '02 film of an alcoholic,
as we sipped 151.

I fell in love with you.

Engrossed in sarees flowing through wind,
the stretch of the drum you played.
Pretending your fingertips were fluid.

Enthralled in the culture of rhythm which launched words
behind
them,
and poetry through the sound of the **real** classical music.
Understanding nothing it pierced my heart with a knife
sharper than ignorance.

I learned to be a woman through the motions of the flick,
of,
the wrist.
The most beautiful woman in the world,

'94.
We shared the date, yet nothing more
other than the love.

I was do-re-mi,
yet the skip of my heart was your fingertips across drumbeats.
We both didn't know the translation.

Bleeding through my soul,
and your rhythm overtaking my body
for life.

Tea.

I was not allergic to anything.
"*Melissa, is very allergic to caffeine. It makes her act so funny.*"

A young me sipped a chocolate milk in the back seat of the car,
spazzing through my mind.
More thoughts than I could ever imagine.
Anxiety reigning me in when allergies were what we told the rest of the world.
What we told myself.

"Oh, well I didn't know you drank coffee."
My teller smiling, trying to control the liquids I drank,
to control the actions of something I seemed to never understand.

My fifth coke,
my fifth embarrassing outrage,
and the forty-fifth time I asked if the door was locked.
My teller began to give me water when all I wanted was the fear of questioning within caffeine.

The thoughts intruding into my brain,
unknowing of why I couldn't let things go.
The caffeine holding on to every mistake,
every unhappy thought,
and the ineffective way I tried to present myself to
all of the hating baristas.

My love's mother handed me a tea,
steeped with what felt warm
and unfamiliar.
Unique and wonderous all at the same time—
a cup.
She looked with caring soul irises,
"I put some milk in it for you."

I gulped the tea down and the caffeine produced in the right hands,
was able to calm the mind
of a girl who once was allergic.

Latte.

In grade nine,
Mrs. Whatever asked everyone to go 'round,
including and speaking their heritage.

Getting to me,
I looked at the ground hating speaking up. Everything I said
was more pounds of funny to those boys.
Always the creator of the joke,
avoiding becoming the butt of it.

"I guess I'm Italian,"
looking at me after I uttered what she reached an offense to.
"Well, and American,"
she darted back.

My mistake in thinking I didn't belong in a town of people
who considered
American-Italian,
more important than just Italian heritage.

Visibly,
milk.
Asking what soap I used,
"Your skin is like cream, like milk."
Like nothing,
when we destroy the beautiful *mother* who gives it to us.

He now touches my face with his skin holding nothing,
but love.
Never slaughtering the animal whose innocence creates
the milky white complexion,
of a girl with red inside.

Chai, Tea, Latte

Never made logic in the world with fascinations as definitions.
Chai chai milk.
Tea tea milk.

A mistake by those who define it or try to create a mixture,
in which nothing can be created.

You gave me chai,
your mother gave me tea,
and you love my Italian latte.

Nightlights

Night lights flickered as cars drove down the long,
and winding valley.
Through the backwoods where you'd swear you'd hear a banjo—
delivering vibes.

The flickering would slip into my eyesight,
as I was drifting off through the midnight hours.
I was scared to death of what death even was.
Changing in the hallways just to avoid shutting the door,
fear of being vulnerable to the demons within the darkness.

Slumbering with lights on with television programs,
drifting in and out of conscious.
I was finding no hope in the darkness of the woods.
I moved.

Sirens,
alarms,
any people.
The traffic of the world around me,
alleviating the fear that a monster hiding under the bed
could attack me.

Realizing too late that no matter the lights,
simply closing my eyes—
I was always thinking in dark places.
They'd trap me in the room with candle light blown out.

Closing eyes,
breathing in the peace of the inside,
I never found the light.

Embracing Agni in the pitch dark,
I slept in stillness.
Forever in the truth of being alone. And being okay with it.

He Lies in Bed

He's lying in bed.
Cuddled up between two blankets,
we sit on the couch drinking the tea.
The coffee drips between two lips.
The lips he kissed last night.

So adult.

He's lying in bed.
Dreaming of things I cannot see,
couldn't see, at one time sought not to see—
blinded by rose tinted privilege.
Yet, he smiles throughout his slumber,
all tucked away
beneath the blankets of *Home.*

He's lying in bed.
Feeling my fingertips run through his hair, simple smile.
I tuck,
tuck,
tuck the blankets underneath him
making him into a small little wrap
of joy.

Hugging with strong arms,
I let him sleep.

He's lying in bed.
I awake
and him in true
innocence,
the childlike notion of freedom.
No matter what his soul could love while dreaming of me.

Little Things

I remember little snaps throughout your insults.
When I asked for a spoon full of soup, and you rolled your eyes.
It was extra-calories and extra-nurturing I was looking for.
Getting mad when I again asked,
"Well, I'll just have some of your salad."

The little ways we speak
hold up when big hatred for our body,
our mind,
reacts with the impulse of the universe.
I no longer eat
with no yearning.

Protection.
It was your main want yet protecting me from the little insults
you yourself might have said to *yourself*.
Why?

He reacts with the sun,
so bright and beautiful.
Glowing the sparkle of
jet black hair,
"you hungry? a biryani? a pizza?"

Asking me why I love him
I reply,
It's the little things.

The Bonfire

Snap,
and crackle,
and wisps of red flit into the summer air
as the mosquitos have their own plan of action.

Timberland trees,
among feet, all of us.
Congregating into the forest where parents did not go.

Light it up,
toke up the sunscreen,
for the people among us were celebrating youthfulness
into the trees.

Burning.
Up.

The taste of beers symbolically no top shelf.
The smiles of nothingness,
and minimum wage of being friends
in the woods.

Glowing from the inside,
I would enjoy the simplicity now of what gave my face a burn.
Understanding today there is no going back
to gristle,
unless I plant my own,
Tree.

Café Crème

Loneliness comes swift and furious,
down hallways unexpectedly.
It doesn't count the doorways or wonder if,
"Did you invite me because you were forced?"

It comes in the form of donuts,
of two dinners,
and of bobby pins
scratching deeply into my skin when my hair still laid in my eyes.
Hiding behind glasses it creeped along the floorboards,
into folded hands at my heart wondering why,
just why?

Woking up with slumber filled eyes,
placing the cup at the edge of my makeup studio—
I sipped,
I sipped.
The drink going down and energized into addiction.

My father placed a cup of coffee beside on my dresser
each morning.

When night prayers turned into morning thanks,
and empty lunches turned into tables with others;
addicted to the same beverage,
the pills turned into beans.

Consistency of nature in my eyes as they opened
to a world,
where loneliness was allergic to the caffeine
I used to avoid.

The Sun Came Over the Hills

My family would lose power,
if a snowstorm hit the right nuts and bolts.
No power,
No water,
No television,
No radio.

Hot dogs burning on the fire.
Corn between elements
heating up in the old-fashioned way—
I would read a book with a candle.

Silence in the country
is compared to the silence of the white noise in the city.

The coyotes clawing up the ground trying to find an animal
scarier than they were.
As was I,
reading Jane Austen seven years before I understood why
it was in such a tight,
bonded
book
jacket.

Calling for updates, hearing that the lines were down,
we'd have to wait for another forty million years.
The power would always be out,
as tight waisted men in suits in the city
suggested,
"Have you tried turning it off again?"

The men with their suit jackets at the office
regulated that it was the farmer's fault.
"The lines were a convenience,

just like the teachers,
the programs,
the sports with no lights.

You had plants, well, no you got rain.
The Northeast was where you CHOSE to live
now wasn't it?"

Men with boots and dirt, men with ties.
Men. Men. Men.
We played card games when we could no longer turn on the TV.

The lights flickering,
meaning the blue were out there working just to define what it meant to put in
a hard day's work.

Filling tubs with water just to bathe.
I noticed that growing up in the dark
while reading with just a candle,
we never really had the power.
The power of the men;
men, men, men
in tight suits
ever really turned on.

The Life I've Always Wanted

At 14,
I felt done with the life I've always wanted.
I'd wake up praying that I might have arose in England
as my travel magazines spread across my floor
reminded me that I had never been,
up in the air.

"*Living*" in
Paris,
Rome,
Seville,
for months being shoved to take the ticket from my pocket
and enjoy peanuts and plastic glasses of tomato juice.
I enjoy the times I cried
for Europe after bleeding in my shoes running through Villa
Borghese,
Luxembourg Gardens
and back to the nurseries of home.

As the wheels touched down
in the fatherland,
eating olives from the bushes reminding myself,
why was I still sad?
After waking up in a different place I was still confined to the
same bones,
with slashes across them.

There was no magic,
no glitter in the air like I thought there would be.
There was no romance in the air,
or when I said ciao,
I still sounded ignorant to the fact that it was no longer my
language.
Never had been, words belong to their special bounds.

I was butchering it still eating beef
in the kitchen.

The life I've always wanted,
I drew on postcards in fourth grade as teachers would remark,
"Where do you see yourself in ten years?"
Here.
This is what I thought I wanted in mindless dreams,
that's all they were, just dreams.
I still can't believe the reality,
of when I woke up in where I wanted to be.

It wasn't right.
It didn't fit.
I had hair missing on the side of my head, thinking that the
mirror
of the slopes of Palermo could have
warmed my curiosity.

Yet, I was always living the life I wanted.

Because it wasn't the travels,
the red tomato juice in cups,
or the pizza with the thick crusted bread my ancestors ate.

I didn't.

I ended up across the lake in the closest arena,
the place I was meant to be.

I was always living the life I wanted.
The beauty of even the town back in the leaf piles,
for I was living Melissa's life.
I was living for Melissa.

Krumkill

Today I woke up,
breathing in the oxygen you gave me.
A tree planted 18 years ago with bark aged against the wind
of the words of the people who weren't planters.

It never broke.
Growing up to the sky, reaching out to the sun where the hills
roll over to the village.
I could barely walk to the next house.

Free and open air,
my branches, leaf to sky.

Yet how do I repay the Earth—
by giving dark through my energy?

I Forgive, Myself

Yet, I don't forgive you.
Not forget,
because that's not what you wanted,
I don't think.

Yet, I forget you.
Even when I was brave to speak out against the actions
of your man-called *primal* nature,
disgusting, I won't forget. Never, I know your name
even when anxiety won't let me shake it.

Yet, I forgive my beautiful body.
Six years of a grudge can weight years off of the holder.
I benefit nothing from carrying the horrors,
and the pain of seeping into unconsciousness.
This beautiful frame holds none of the cells' touch you pressed
on me.
New form.
I won't forget,
because I will never.
Your grasp burnt into my body waking up the next morning.
Every morning,
wondering if I ever did something so wrong,
the universe was tempting to tell me a message.

"Drink less,
wear pants,
lose weight."

Yet, I won't forget that face.
Staring into the retinas of the man who took
everything and nothing with him.
Assault meant I kept myself intact,
but gave me a horrific memory of being female.

I forgive innocence, my child, me the virgin girl.
Until my words become so strong they create weight on your consciousness.
Until, the strength of my love for myself
weighs so strong on you,
you'll scream NO to the sky.

And I will hear you.
Accepting no as an answer. No as the final answer, consenting.

Consenting your choice of words,
but never forgetting to let go of the captures I've endured.
And never,
never forgiving.

I Forgive, My Teller

We laugh.
Today across the phone, I tell you of my day to day,
I realize,
we are no longer so different.

Commonality of happiness.
Comparing our thoughts on how we cook,
we clean,
I no longer make pies, but vegetables from you.
Recipes you said were like experiments,
when I dissected their sentences. Burnt, fire alarm always on.

We smile as I remark what I thought I would never say,
"I miss you."

Times come and go,
I've grown into something, not woman not child.
A something in between and I notice the way we both clean
our glasses the same way.
I sweep just like you,
common traits.
Like suffering.

I forgive.
I laugh at animation.
I cry at horror movies, still afraid to sleep with the lights off.
I was always this person among you,
you just didn't see it. Didn't see beyond a child.

I forgive the screaming, and the hiding of my diary under the bed.
I give you now my words.
Do with them as you should or as you will.
I hold no torch to your actions,
lifting the reigns off of the leash.

Now, I can see you,
lonely.
Our old friend in the dusk of the rainstorm,
snowstorm,
He awaits all.
No matter the age. Woman or little one.

I was never a human
without loneliness.
For it doesn't exist.

I see you now,
not through you.
We are women even though friend was never our adjective.

Changing my name, but I will always be the daughter of the
dirt-ly paved roads.
Still work, but not perfectly.
The daughter of the trees swinging in the distance
reacting with the winter of your insults.
I understand the comments today
protection under the disguise of
hurt.

To my teller,
I accept the childhood I was never given,
expecting nothing to retrieve it.
It's gone now.

There is Beauty in the Leaves

I was always afraid of dying until the only death I knew,
were people who had taken it into their own prayed hands.

It turned into a constant fear of eating this,
drinking that.
The lead of the pipes leading the worries in my brain.
I was trapped in my own thoughts in the grid system of the city
I ended up in.

Dying,
was I living?
No.

There is beauty in the leaves.
In front of my face as the trees outside my window,
would sway back and forth.
Back and forth.
With the sun beaming off the vertebrae of the leaf,
fallen to the ground.

How could we die to end up in a place where trees do not root?

I was a warrior.
A fleck of the window
flowing through the air.
I missed the house of my lover's family
even if family wasn't born with me.
I was watered as their child,
my feet sprouting into the ground of chosen love.

I was a whisper sprinkled on the tongue of the people
who grew up with me,
who cut me down,
and who didn't see that my dormant state was just me

taking a break.
I grew stronger, thicker branches, and thicker bark.

There is beauty in the leaves.

As they flitter to the ground leaving the tree bare in the winter,
"that tree is dead."
It wasn't.
Life's greatest mystery,
of how the trees, like seasons play pranks on us all.

Childhood my winter,
I was now full bloom.
Spring had risen, I had risen,
without a name to my glory—palms up.

We are all nature.
Mother Auntie residing in all of us.
Spirit didn't need a name,
I learned that now.
It was too much to give a name,
even I was never
Melissa.
Missy
Myself.

There is beauty in all of us.
We flow from tree to home,
laying down our history to future.
So that for our next life,
we shall simply call it Spring.

I AM NOT YET A WOMAN

I am not yet a woman,
by the standards that we believe.

I was not yet a child.
I was not yet a female,
I was not yet one singular motion.
For you to tell me,
for why?

I am spirit inside.
Flaming forward with sparkle in these eyes.
I will be spirit again,
if only you feel the wrath of my symptoms.

I am everything,
you see when you pray in the dark.
I am everything I always was.

I am child.
I am woman.
I am nothing, too,
for the non-believer.

Seeing my reflection with my eyes slammed shut,
the radiation of truth.

I am everything in this world,
and
you could never name me.

I Like to Wear Florals

Born in the wilderness of dandelions and juniper trees,
I had dirt up my nose, and mud in my sneakers.
I didn't wear dresses,
jean shorts.

Rompers, and romping around the corn fields,
it was a protest shirt from *You're Always Gonna Be 21*,
(you're not)
size 17 shorts from the store with meat and clothing,
and a belt made from pleather.

Hiding for years,
I dressed tough.
Suppressing behind septum piercings,
and half shaved heads.
Green hair and metal combat boots in 90 Fahrenheit,
now 30 Celsius weather.

One time referring to myself,
"a canvas of metal," picturesque of art.
Most like the demolitions of the big city,
as blood pierced jewelry hung from the body
of an inward dead flower.
Running away from society's notion of
pretty.

But . . .
I met the love of my life in a pink skirt,
and like the child who ran within dandelion fields,
I planted seeds of self-growth and self-worship.
Watering inside organs with the streams of love,
who felt rain pour from the heart which was once dry as desert.

I fell in love with nature again,
whom was slashed and burnt to a crisp.
I fell in love with pollen again,
as bumblebees respect their Queen.
Me.

And now I only wear florals of pink and purple bright,
blooming from a strong lotus flower within.
As now the mud the trespasser gave me,
it is the foundation of my bloom.
The strongest of female, loved by his—
the Queen dressed in a floral cocktail gown
unafraid of getting it dirty.

Running Through Cunningham Park

Everyday a long six miles meant to me the key to eat
whatever I wanted.
Unhealthy addiction at its finest,
and yet the high of turning the trail four times over was a
glorious robusto.

Run and pace and run and pace,
stop for the streetlight.
Now jog up and down,
those people are staring—let them stare.

At 10 PM at night, running down Union Turnpike,
Jamaica, Queens,
Fresh Meadows, Queens,
or whichever you said to show off in Canada.
I ran through Queens, nah change it to Brooklyn.

Lights dangled from the broken posts,
and there was no looking into the forbidden forest of the park
filled with love
and old men softball during the day.
At night hiding the burning red eyes of treacherous pro-life beasts
and five-tongued politicians.
It was time to turn home,
and run fast through the traffic of luring lookers,
my own contaminated fears.

One day giving in,
fuck it.

Just run.

The worries of childhood,
the worries of dating,

the worries of my body,
and the food in which it craved since birth.

Just *run* through the park at night.
Just <u>run</u> through the park at night.
Just **run** through the park at night.

I lived to jog by Lake Ontario this morning.
A privilege to shine by the waters clear,
and to hear panting from the lungs below.

For every woman runs through the park at night,
to test and survive the miles we didn't design for our own
bodies.

And I got to leave it all behind in the dust of my awakening,
and in the dust of the strength to propel me forward.
Fearing the night—I will once again need to run through the park
of my memories.

WHAT DID YOU DO THIS WEEKEND?

I saw you like the picture.
You know that I know that I know you know you saw the picture,
of the eggs I made on a Saturday morning,
but called it Brunch.
I know you know what I did.

"So, what did you do this weekend?"
(Hmph)

I went to hear music and it sounded off-key in the way
that Edie's boyfriend would twiddle with the strings,
just right and raw.
I saw a DJ,
I went to the park's freshly mowed grass, and
I made love to the husband I met three years ago, and
whose lips taste like melted marshmallows and comfort.
I had a drink, took a puff,
pet a doggo,
and watched the latest children's movie to cry about my own
humanity,
and how I can't connect with loved ones even as their youth
is escaping them through multiplying cells.
I plotted the extremities of the universe,
and why have our calls never been answered?
I prayed at the foot of my bed and asked Krishna to appear
before me,
so that I could understand the guilt I feel when I was abused
by a teller who told me to grow when I wasn't even bleeding.
A period of wrist slits, and now do you love me?

So, I said, "Uhhhh, nothing really. Just stayed in the city."
You liked my self portrait of filters and lights,
and I know that you know,
I didn't do anything like worthy special.

On Being Honest

My honesty is a lie these days,
as I can barely call the self, myself.
I was what I thought you wanted me to be,
as everything amounted of myself was . . .
my child.

Favourite colour,
gendered.
Favourite music,
what my elder listened too,
and favourite movie was one I hid in the basement
to try to grow up
within two and a half hours.
Basing life on fiction, and fiction on believing this
was to be my narrative.

Afraid to say the truth of my heart's beating,
I don't like to drink beer as a country girl.
The shock in the city folk's faces as a young girl unafraid
to admit the drinks a poison
to safety of heart and body.
Two-dollar wine I swigged in my purse in Paris,
but a married 24-year-old, you can't be perfect in the path
of womanhood.
A young woman too young,
an old woman too old.
And a woman all together,
too much.

I had years of what you call your early twenties,
as all Millennials recall the '90s to lasting over three decades.
All '90s children reminisce of the time before every second was
liked
in real time.

Every outside adventure of internet fame, glory,
and connection,
simply lost to the motherboard.

My honesty these days is a lie,
as it's simply easy to project the truth through screens of misrepresentation.
Who was I?
I was all of the worst things you thought of me,
hidden away within your likes.

That was the truth.

The Funny One

Class clown, class megaphone,
hilarious, and down to Earth.
The shield of a mushroom haircut, and *overweight* pounds of,
"depressed I ate the ice cream scoop, eat the entire bowl."

Funny.

Jokes turn to lies, and cover ups,
as tragedy plus time can make someone laugh
even though time plus tragedy becomes
those memories you can't escape from.
In real time,
fat-phobic, now you don't believe that's who I was.

The funny one.

"Laugh it off, just a joke."

I had laughed off forty-five pounds of insults,
and comments.
And sexual encounters,
of unwanted fingers who could poke the funny girl,
but I never got the joke.

I wasn't funny,
I was resilient in the world who values my laughter
over my honesty.

So, I stopped laughing,
and those friends of foe left my stand up.
A serious performance of prose with commas,
and honesty to tell you,
I no longer wished to be the butt of the joke.

And it was me in the silence of the mountain,
and it wasn't rough-men
in the silence of powerful protest.

I was funny because of resilience,
but I refuse to accept their wicked laughter
as admiration.

Hyphen

Many times, I was told use the hyphen for a longer—
pause.
The comma was just a slight emphasis on the point
I was trying to make,
and it wasn't working anymore.
People had stopped—
listening to me.

Their idea of me, like an outcast of the streets
where the city lights were masked by my own indecision
of where I was from.
Who was I?
A child in their mind,
a child who hasn't taken their own form—
bears in the forest of can't make up my mind.

Life is the experience we give it—
who defines the one who experiences too much of it?
You blow up with a culture not yours,
if you try to claim the pain you've felt as validation
for your actions.

Was it all worth it?

Rhymes strung together by basic pauses,
and you sit in chairs listening to those who've claimed they've
worked harder—
grinded harder.
They ain't work shit,
and they know it, you know it too.

But who are you?

Other than experiences strung together by commas,
experiences strung together by slight pauses of pain.
You have no time,
and no heart any longer to pause for toxic people and the—
hyphens for which they cause.

The Dichotomy of the Rite Aid Nail and Those Purchased from Shopper's Drug Mart

One.
The Rite Aid nail kit purchased alongside the:
- Booze, of all kinds, mainly Tecate.
- Nail glue, falling off easily when ripping off long hair extensions and text books. Also, you were opening cans of Tecate. Sometimes with your teeth.
- Tampons.

Two.
The Shopper's Drug Mart nail kit were purchased for two things:
- Scratching your lover's legs as you discussed the lines of creativity, thought, the perception of time, and Wu Tang.
- Acrylics were finally mainstream, stolen, enough to lie about where these nails had come from.

Three.
Both nails were shitty drug store nails,
waving them around in the air as your cardio was,
Burn Three Billion Calories in Thirty Minutes.
Four.
These nails represented the nervous child you couldn't tame, as a 12-year-old bit off her nails waiting for each class to be over. One day crying out of school, ran through the hallways and fell into the snowbank on lower dirt Hilton Road, as you call your parents to pick you up from the gas station. The bullies didn't care your manicure was a French Tip you saw on magazines, you were reading *what whoever was wearing*, as they were reading nothing. You traded up to the free magazine sent with newspaper, which let you in on the emo trend, a razor blade was the cover. A middle school lifestyle was born, already fantasizing of the tattoos you'd use to cover your wrist scars.
Five.
They were pink and sparkly.

Downtown

Too much love for the downtown—
you forget about rolling hills and inequality of the . . .
literally everything.

((Too much love for the hip bars, the cool clubs, everything about it, yeah so fresh death. Dying from claustrophobia. Engulfed inside something too small for big personalities saying that they are more than a small fish in a big pond. I was a whale, big enough to know it, but you don't have to own the world, to see it. And most importantly, you don't take the selfie.))

City streets were gonna fix all the problems
of you not having a family,
but ain't ya just some hick with corn beneath her tooth?
Let me ask you how you gonna get to the beach when it's hot?
The only way Queens got rain was when the hurricane came
to blow it over.
Toronno, ocean lake filled with **uncooked** chicken eggs.
Take a two-hour subway ride,
and walk the rest of the way along the oceanside . . .
count your blessings and your precious downtown.

Kicked out, to kick it back in.
Those don't know the prison when they're the ones creating
the bars,
but enjoy your thirty-dollar martini in your condo
built with paper.

And your flashing lights within the deejay music you enjoy
mixing,
as you didn't know a hick could travel the world.
Married: he's my best friend.

How many downtowns did I need to call home—
how many apartments filled with mold—
how many spiders crawling in between my sheets—
how many "what street do you live on?" did
I need to answer for you to know;
I'm alive.

Downtown doesn't mean forward thinking,
just tunneling in the cycle of those who came before us.
Limiting the Earth—sectioning it off wealth, power,
and who has to pay cover.

I wasn't broke,
but with this, I just wasn't buying.
Dollars you didn't see in my hand,
you just thought I was poor.

Downtown.

Wedding

"People who throw those big weddings, well they're just throwing them for themselves. They don't care about family."
"Well, don't you just want a big party? Something small we can throw, ya know a party?"
"Saree, not lehenga."
"White, not cream."
"Oh, you're not serving steak at your wedding?"
"From what I've understood, there's not a lot of structure in that type of wedding?"
"It's just so vain to throw something, you're already married, it doesn't matter."

One conscious stream of not caring for their child,
hidden behind morality,
and a higher purpose of saving money.
How dare you want to be happy?
As all those who stared at me,
would know my Lady hands covered in the blood of
never having a party.
My love traditional, being mistaken once again for
taking away my own choice.

Progress: Definition:
"advancement."
Advancement of my happiness or
your opinion of how I should female?

Support?
No, I didn't need it in money, career,
but this . . .
this was something else, a lack of sympathy for the human
emotion.

After all of that loss of innocence,
I had found someone to make me smile.
Make me laugh,
make me come, hither to
make me respond to something other than terrifying melodrama.

"Just something small."

Thinking of it as small,
when my happiness could be described with the adjective as
small.
I am space within this everlasting vastness.

And the loss of innocence finally taking the form,
of conditional love and their responses.

If you want something in this beautiful world,
you have to find someone who will force you
to do it your fucking-self.
Whether it be the inward narrator,
or the one who inspires that inward love.

And I will wear a red garment,
as the blood of my innocence will celebrate the love of
my life.
Dripping in romance,
and He in Guyana gold.

Experience

There are many things I wish I hadn't experienced,
but more things I wish I never said.

"I'm glad it happened to me . . ."
"I think I learned something, don't drink, don't wear shorts,
don't get puffin'."
"It was my fault."

A child who's glad she's no longer a child.
A little girl who no longer felt like a woman.
As you nodded and agreed.
You didn't do anything—
but you talked like you did.

I'll never forgive that.

Then I swallowed your words in the way that I said them—
but more in the way that they were received.
I lashed onto those angry pellets and bullets of hate I spread;
a bird doesn't worry where its shits fallen.
Fire energy radiating, as I was freezing in my heart,
so cold it felt hot like hell.

But that's what the weak mind doesn't get.

You're not just what you've been through.
Why you can't just pass on the things you've done,
but the words you've said to those who haven't even—
touched you.

And the things I said to those whose fists hit me,
whose words never slapped me with a tender grace,
as I never connected with the fighter against me.
How it was Queens that shaped me,

the F train and RuPaul 2018.
I wasn't no more a child,
and I wasn't an experienced adult through actions
and those trainings of my own.

Who was I, but these poems of what I have done?

I had said enough in this lifetime for the hellish gates
to open me up.
And it was her words that shattered me,
with those "grow up . . ."
and his words that sewed me back together
again.

People got it all wrong.

Didn't need all of the alphabet, didn't need all of the periods.
Didn't need anything, but the truth in the words
and how you speak them.

Blessed my truth,
wouldn't take a lifetime to say.
That was growing older,
that was growing wiser.

Losing my innocence to the prose of these poems,
and the commas.
Because my life wasn't taking pauses of long elongated silent
grammar,
I had already experienced those days and passed through
somehow.

All of those hyphens,
all of those periods.
It was all worth learning.
And I won't forget the stanzas I've already completed,
but look forward to the couplets I create out of my joy—
my love.

For life was onward,
and it was going,
going,
going . . .

Sunday Vibes, Sunday Morning

Curled up with a good book,
a love story, ya' know?
The epic tale
of crossing over rocks—they made to keep the love.
You look at me
from across the duvet sitting in silence,
hair ruffled like *high fashion.*
You play games through a virtual reality,
as I listen to the sword play.

Clink.
Clink.
Clink.
Slice.

Sunday vibes,
my hands to my heart.
Just feeling the calming tea of breath hit my lips.
Inner and outer,
feeling the morning dew inside of my—
skin.
That sweet smell of rain we crave it,
but it sure does make me cry.

In the crisp morning of the Autumn breeze,
it was coming—one single leaf falls off the tree.
I get scared,
as I always did you pointed out.

And it wasn't in whistles,
bells,
organs,
or guitars.

Just clinks upon clinks,
that I knew something more than just love was in the room.

And Sunday vibes,
you are my temple.

True Self

The time of blaming childhood was
over.
It was time to move on in the grand scope
of whatever this linear time was,
but I experienced those childhood memories every second
upon falling asleep.

But the true self,
who was she?
Who was the one
inside me?

Inspirations from those who touched my hands,
heart, and him who touched my eyes
when I see him after days of longing for pressure.

True self,
I don't believe so.
The only truth I knew was when I stopped
so hard to find me.
I was there in the darkness of those childhood
memories.
Waiting to grow.

You Can't Be Sad Over Nothing

As I sat in rooms alone praying to something in the universe,
you told me aloud many times,
"You just can't be sad over nothing."

Telling myself this
over and over again,
becoming a symptom of the way I eased myself into triggers.

"You can't just be sad over nothing,"
it was true.
You were right.
Forgetting the fact,
that it wasn't the nothing,
but the who.

I discovered a room in my heart and
it was emptier than the blue skies over country pathways.
And more skittish than the deer in the yard
or the stutter in my throat.

"You can't just be sad over nothing,"
I agree.
It was never nothing,
but the who.

You Were Never

. . . in a scoffed off tone, with rolling eyes in disgust.
I'd use that r word to really describe the feeling not the action.
Law claims that women have no ownership of their,
body—
their flowers,
their expression of how it feels.
To lose control in that place forever which would now feel lost.

You were assaulted,
by definition. Written by who?
Sexual attack,
classified the feeling of losing oneself.
A diagram,
a diagnosis,
a finger,
lips,
but no other.

You were never raped.
Ringing, ringing, ringing,
and subconsciously you say it. Say it out loud now. But, you can't accept it, because that flower buries deep within.

With one phrase to question all of my suffering,
did I even deserve to feel lost? Did she even deserve to feel lost?
Did you?

Who didn't deserve the
trial,
the kits,
and most of all the looks from the pale and male questioners
(always pale),
"Why didn't you just kick him off?"

Taking time out of today's happiness
to remember when she wasn't raped,
no,
attacked.
Only we find power in the words,
that accurately describe the events of the night.

You were never raped.
Lost in technicalities and definitions of legal dominance.

Searching endlessly,
for the words to describe the feeling
of not knowing how to describe the feeling.
Feelings, fluid, and what I still feel.

When all of the definitions,
all of the sentences,
are all quite simply male and pale.

My frame assaulted—
damaging more than just
flowers.
Growing weeds inside to intertwine within my own shame,
only now these words, her own definition. Individually.
I am my words and it is mine.

You were never raped,
yet, my femininity was
taken.

He's Not Your God

"He's not your God,"
He's not.
I am his.

To choose,
you can't.
Sitting as a child praying in silence.
My voice carrying over the gentle hum of the silent,
winter,
even throughout the summer solstice.

Prayers handcrafted,
though time and time again.
They were filtered,
scared to be overheard.

A young self, praying did blood blisters popped—
clasping my hands so hard,
they lost feeling.
Not from faith,
but from the mortality engaged within them.

Replies hidden,
replies gave.

He found me.

Through love,
I found the one who hears my earnest whimpering's and
for answers.
I listen, unmoved by commotion,
spinning all around me.

Breathing in gently
to hear the universe offer me the secret
to the why?
Knowing that I am here,
indefinitely.
"He is not your God,"
no, he isn't.

He is everyone's,
yet more importantly,
is everyone, seen within brown eyes and the Guyanese sun.

Skipping beats for happiness and joy in temple songs.

Prayer beads between my papers,
of Gita stories, the one you gave me with a Haiku you wrote
in its pages.
I was always praying to him,
even if by a different name. Even if by your name.

"He is not your God,"
no, he is not. Yet, I am His.
Yet, I am Yours.

YOU CAN'T STILL BE HUNGRY

"You can't still be hungry,"
I was.

To this day,
the minute I finish something
I think to myself of the next
meal,
country,
event,
position,
next.

The thriving life of feeling more and more starved for
everything around in the spaces between my two hands.
I ate food in place of
books,
company,
and compassion.
While growing up and out in a bigger belly,
I now love my thick thighs.

Hungry,
but more importantly passionate.
To devour the learnings
and passion around me,
I dance to the beat of
fried dough,
while reading the poetry and songs of the place my heart yearns
for with the man,
the love who feeds every appetite.

I was hungry for love
disguised in pints of ice cream,
and calories.
Today I have both,
eating sandwiches with my lover in bed.

I am going to eat
two plates,
two helpings,
two lives in one,
until the next meal,
I share is in the life after this.

I Have Loved You

Déjà,
You.

The feeling I felt walking into temple on 1ST Ave
I knew,
that I had loved you. Some time and place, which had not been the present.

Past tense turning into a present,
I was opening with every kiss.
Every hug,
every handhold that your fingers
were grasping at through centuries.

I have loved you even until tomorrow,
when your skin may look different glows.
I shall appear thicker,
yet my words will still never rhyme.

Comfortable way I wear you on my heart and the way that you speak with not a candid nature,
but just a second nature,
after all.

You,
my rock.
Over time,
over centuries,
over lifetimes we carry,
into diamonds.

I have loved you, and you have loved me.

You're All Grown Up

Years of confusion,
I remember when scoffs were greeted to my childlike mind.
Knowing that at the age of 11,
I was a woman.

"You're all grown up."
A statement to this day I still didn't know if it is good,
or just confusing.

Growing into myself,
I was understanding how to think.
Yet, for me always thinking hatred thoughts for the self.
Wondering if I could have grown up
different,
less than what was considered sideways.

All grown up,
not even close.

The petals were torn,
and the roots were dusty.
Not red of the earth where it meets,
my meditative stand.
My circles of color seem to be all out of sync,
throughout the spine I carried high.
I was growing,
I wasn't yet grown.

The child you screamed at and the child you forced to retreat
into the solidarity of adulthood
was now all too grown
for you to understand.

Hate the child,
miss the adult.

Picking and choosing my age,
I now take the stand.
I now take the reins of the way time is not,
a conducive form of the Universe.

I was all ages.
I was the childlike adult,
whose voice vibrates through the pages.

I will never be grown,
never child,
nor adult,
but always growing.

What Do You Want to Be When You Grow Up

Confusing,
and terrified over the future of what was to come.
Trapped in the anxiety,
of what used to be.

Jobs with dirt under my nails and coffee stains on my shirts,
and the dream that one day I could buy pre-cut groceries.
The Millennial want,
to simply be happy.

Debts ravaging over everything I touch and a piece of lined paper,
costing upwards of fifty
thousand dollars,
times five.

"What do you want to be when you
grow up?"

Not happy—
not content—
not questioning my constant
outcome.

We are more
than just our titles.
We are more
than just what we do.
What we think
and what we hope to accomplish,
more than that.

What we want to be,
holds no holds on us.
I learned the
long way in a short span.

We already are. We are born grown.

The Girl Who Cried Wolf

MRI and brain tumors,
"no, no tell the doctor I need to be seen either today,
or, no tell him today."
Panic inside the tube I asked for,
"ma'am you're going to have to sit still."

Lead poisoning and brain fog,
I know they put something in that take away.
"Oh my god!
It's gluten,
there solved it."
Bread tastes . . .
delicious.

It's this.
This.
That.

Have your tried meditation?
No, but the lactose free milk will make life
WAY easier.

How about yoga?
I think I'm having an aneurism.
Breathe four, hold . . .

Tears and tears of illnesses that never knocked on my door,
and fearing them to come in the night.

We scare them away,
The demons . . .
with silence.

My chest hurts, the pounding of 24 years of worrying
combined with gas from those salt and vinegar chips I had.
You hold me still, and as the girl who cried wolf too many times,
you blew out the fire with your laughter.

That's all the wolf needed—
a good joke, and a lover who would endlessly answer the same
five questions.

Auntie

"Do you want more tea"—
Have I told you that I love you?
As we lay on a carpeted floor, playing and watching tv
with the innocence of the children
we lost within accomplishments,
Auntie brings me one more snack,
cream included.

And saag, and cheese roll, and bake, and a story of how
the autumn leaves looked in front of Macy's.
I once auditioned to be the elf at Christmas time, didn't get it.
Buying bargain books in the library at Bryant Park, and how
when I didn't get published, I sat in the stacks and cried,
took her son—my love
back to buy books and a tote bag.
She the original poet.

Strength is perceived in those who grow it, and she gave me the strength of all of the world. Within, "do you want more food? what do you want to take?"

And she taught me to tie a saree, in her saree, the one off her back, and she gave it to me without thinking twice, and I don't know how much love you must have in your heart to give the saree off your back to the girl who looks like those who questioned why you're wearing it to begin with. Long Island Women, and their questions with ignorance.

Strength.

Fighting to find a home for yourself because you needed to,
the restless spirit of a wanderer and
the mother you became,
both parents in one.

To say love within a Sunday night meal, and the bells
at morning and night,
you looked at me, and said "family."
You chose me, and I fell in love with the feeling of having
a carpet, and I regret every day I didn't touch your feet at first
meeting you.

Because you were my auntie,
and I was your child.

Equanimity

Every meditation begins within walking senses,
and pools of little leaves tapping the waters.
Watch the rings begin to grow,
as hearts grew, while you were on one knee.
Walking miles to the coffee shop one morning, you at work.
Equanimity.

Her name
Santosh, waiting for an apple fritter, we both in gym clothes
from the run.
Looking at me she gazed,
"I do not know English well,
but I know my own better than you.
Two languages."

Candidly without shame, as a powerful woman she taught me.
"Could you help me write an email?"
A smile I won't forget,
as all want to love and be happy,
all other's do too.
"Writer," I gleamed.

She with eyes of pool depth,
remarking on how she needed no one, but a quick thing.
"Could you write my life story?"
Equanimity.

Life. Story.

We sat in the booth of the coffee shop from over there,
from over even farther,
as I fixed the WiFi on her phone, it was calming technology
of wading lakes.

Waiting for our husbands,
as rushed red struck through her scalp like
atoms reclaiming their form. And my red soon enough,
just planning needed.

She placed hand to my hand and the balances of two,
wanting love
and memoirs.

Doshi,
she told to me to call her,
was my first Canadian friend,
neither of us born in Canada.
Imprinting her beauty, grace, and balance to a stressed out,
unemployed writer.
Her life now mixing with my story.

As my path led me to the woman of mystery,
she brought me a double milk—double more milk
and my child's future middle name.

Just as we want to be remembered,
just as we want to be written.
Equanimity in a coffee shop.

Bittersweet

There is something to be said about longing in the way that I longed for you for years, upon years before meeting you for only a slight moment. I didn't know it was you, until I saw it for myself: realization.

I had written poems in your name, in the ways I had written songs without your initials. But that longing for lost time with you, that is the comforting thoughts of a locked door prison.

All those years we will not get back—the wanting. The waiting. And finally, you.

With brown eyes staring into hazel of my own, you were already inside me. Green eyes with innocence and envy pierced by your skin.

And it was worth it, the time of suffering waiting for you. The sweetest nectar, the darkest poison of being lonely. When we first met...after all of those years, I knew it was you. To prove not to look back with blood tinted glasses, but remember how much I felt alone—was fixed.

For when I was waiting to love you, I was learning
to love myself.

And I reminisce of how that suffering—created the strongest love I've ever known in the nostalgia of meeting you . . . and it was all worth it.

You, Raksha, May Rest with The Devil

You, demon may rest with your maker,
as I may with mine, thoughts on who it is? Up to the public,
or my own heart wishes of love and light in November.

Yet, you may sit with what I can remember red eye looking,
staring,
glaring into my hazel innocent eyes as you did,
monster.

For you may rest with your maker,
as I may with mine.
I know deep into my diyas whom that might be,
even if I learned to pray from my husband's side of the family.
It's not in my blood.

As you remember the face lying bare-naked on the floor,
sister, mother, daughter . . . no, of course not. No face at all.
Remember these words as silver emits from all of my arms,
my eyes red, my lips. Stone silent. I shall throw no stones,
even if I deserve to.
All of them as Mother Nature, Mother Mary and I shall embody
the Mother. Remember this girl, these arms, and I now with
your shocked face women of all we come together.
Saying no to the water thrones,
this eve sleeps upon her serpent
offering all of our weapons as one.

Say what you say, I've written it all before.
"You're not a real Hindu,
You're not a virgin Catholic!"
. . . But you, Raksha, may rest with the devil.

A Letter to My Fourteen-Year-Old Self

My child, yes you are still a child.
No, don't grow up too fast, thinking that womanhood is to be chased and lost.
It's already in you, just you wait and see.

My child, don't worry. As worrying will become the
core of your existence at points, you will worry about even your own name.
Written on the tops of pages you've had for decades, worry into a chasm of confusion.
Don't.

My child, be.

Be whatever it is at the time you want, and you don't know it, how likely you will grow.
Within faith, within loves, within drinks from the gas station,
and within these poems you started to write,
there are some still under your bed in the forest.

Enjoy.
Relish.
Decorate.

And forgive.

And tear them all to bits with the words you craft together.

Because you my child,
will live on forever in these words as time stands still. I can still remember the laughter of drives to Vermont, Barrie, and Toronto. You are your own words, lifted out of your lips to the page, and cast aside the ones named about you.

For you are the child,
and I love you.
Always.

Today Is My Birthday

A year older, year wiser.
Reflecting on the wisdom of a child,
pretending to wear the mask of a sage.
Jokes.

Today is my birthday.
The day I saw **His** eyes perk up when he handed me breakfast
in our bed.
I see Him,
in him.

Knowledge and power are too different things
for the endings they seem to tell.
Surrounded by books I was, with glasses shattered
right down the middle.
All of the secrets of the world there for me,
but blurriness of my ignorant nature to see it.

He hands me bifocals with his heart.
And the clearer the love for him,
the more I can read the texts.
Life makes a little more sense when you are being hugged.
Even when it's your own two arms.

The present is always vanishing.
Always.
Grasping out to tangible air,
as I thought that it would fill my soul.

You can't love yourself,
when you're unaware of the love you need, the love just for you.
Trying on fake clothing or jeans that don't fit,
your heart either squeezing it too tight or not at all.

It was never pain.
Anything of it.

Thinking back to memories that make my own head shake
inside of my skull.
It was never your own soul as malicious,
it was never a lesson to be learned.
I left my town because of the boy,
to go to a college,
to meet a girl,
to meet a girl,
who would date some guy, who would introduce me
to the man I call my one.

I was never in the wrong place,
no wrong thought.
Or worry.
Or book too overread.
I was always on track,
running in circles while the Mother guided my soul to where
it needed to remain.

I was right.
I was always right.
I was the one, the strength for myself, the one for me too.

For even though I tried, I remember . . .
I was never a child.

Acknowledgements

Chris Needham and Now Or Never Publishing for giving this collection a home.